THE
ERIE CANAL

by
LINDA THOMPSON

Newbridge

The Erie Canal
ISBN 1-4007-4158-0

Written by Linda Thompson

Published by Newbridge Educational Publishing,
A Haights Cross Communications Company
11 East 26th Street, New York, NY 10010
www.newbridgeonline.com

Title Page: *The remains of the original lock of the Erie Canal in Pitts, New York*

PHOTO CREDITS: Courtesy of Allan Harris: Title Page; Courtesy City of
Rochester, New York: page 35; Courtesy Columbia University: page 18; Courtesy
Corps of Engineers Great Lakes and Ohio River Div.: page 10; Mural by C.Y.
Turner (1905) in DeWitt Clinton High School, New York: page 31; Courtesy Gary
Gold/Rensselaer Polytechnic Institute: page 43; Courtesy Larry Myers: pages 28,
34; Courtesy Library of Congress, Prints and Photographs Division: pages 9, 11,
14, 16, 21, 38-39; Library of Congress, Rare Book and Special Collections
Division: page 36; Courtesy NASA: page 15; Courtesy National Parks Service:
pages 21, 22, 24, 34, 45; Courtesy New York Public Library: page 19; Courtesy
New York Public Library, Phelps Collection of Historical Prints: page 5; Courtesy
New York State Archives: pages 27, 37; Courtesy New York State Library: pages
13, 41; Courtesy Rochester Municipal Archives: page 26; Courtesy Rochester
Museum & Science Center, The Albert R. Stone Negative Collection: page 42;
Courtesy Rohm Padilla: pages 6, 8; Courtesy of TR's Eerie Postcards: page 38;
Courtesy University of Rochester Library: pages 20, 28, 29, 33; Courtesy U.S.
Fish and Wildlife: pages 12, 25; Courtesy U.S. Geological Survey: page 17;
Courtesy U.S. Senate Archives: page 7

10 9 8 7 6 5 4 3 2 1

TABLE OF CONTENTS

Chapter I: CONNECTING WITH THE HINTERLANDS

Only 20 years after it became independent, the United States gained a region that doubled the country's size. And barely 50 years later, it reached across immense plains and towering mountain ranges to touch the Pacific Ocean. One

Many mountain ranges, such as the Marble Mountains of California, were some of the obstacles in the way of American expansion.

early step that helped this rapid expansion succeed was a series of improvements in transportation. Before the coming of the railroads, pulling barges along canals was the logical way to move heavy loads. The Erie Canal, America's first major canal, had an enormous impact on New York State's economy.

Horses and mules were used to walk the lengths of the canals while pulling barges loaded with cargo.

When the year 1803 began, the United States of America had only 17 states and one large **territory** surrounding the Great Lakes. Most of the five and a half million Americans lived along the eastern edge of a huge undeveloped continent. Georgia was the southernmost state, and the western border of the country was the Mississippi River. But by the end of 1803, President **Thomas Jefferson** had purchased the vast and unknown Louisiana Territory. More land was quickly acquired. In 1846, defining the

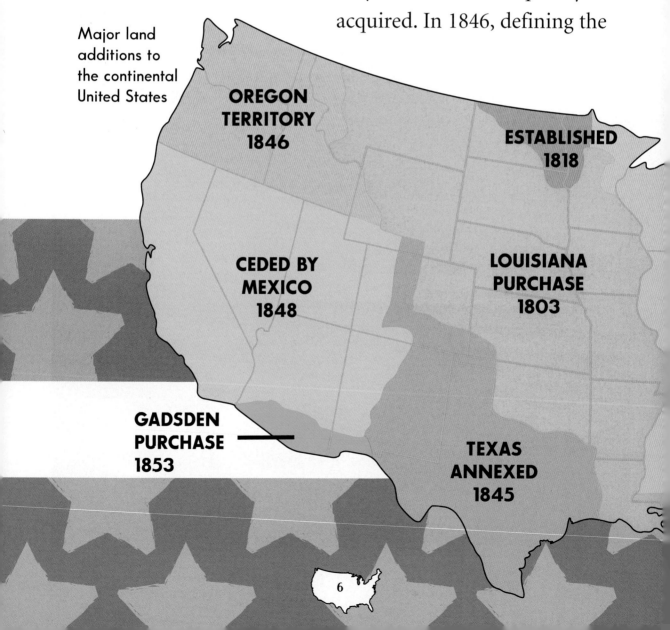

Major land additions to the continental United States

OREGON
TERRITORY
1846

ESTABLISHED
1818

CEDED BY
MEXICO
1848

LOUISIANA
PURCHASE
1803

GADSDEN
PURCHASE
1853

TEXAS
ANNEXED
1845

boundary with Canada made the Pacific Northwest part of the United States. By 1848, the country had added Florida and California, as well as Texas and the Southwest. Another small addition in 1853, the Gadsden Purchase, formed today's **continental** United States in size and shape, not counting Alaska.

President Thomas Jefferson

The challenge of exploring all of this newly acquired territory was immense. But Americans were equal to the challenge. By 1869, a **transcontinental** railroad linked the 3,500 miles (5,633 km) or more of wilderness between the two coasts. The land suddenly became more accessible to explorers, settlers, and people bringing supplies and mail. And there were nearly six times as many Americans as when the century began. People had not only explored and settled much of the new land, but also had made it easier to transport goods and communicate with each other "from sea to shining sea."

UNITED STATES PRIOR TO 1803

CEDED BY SPAIN 1819

Several developments were crucial to this extraordinary and rapid growth. New York State's construction of the Erie Canal linked the busy Atlantic coast with the "**hinterlands**," making people in the Great Lakes region less likely to break away from the United States. And although it took a century to realize the original vision, completion of the Erie Canal made New York the leading state in both population and prosperity.

Map showing the route of the Erie Canal from the Hudson River to Lake Erie

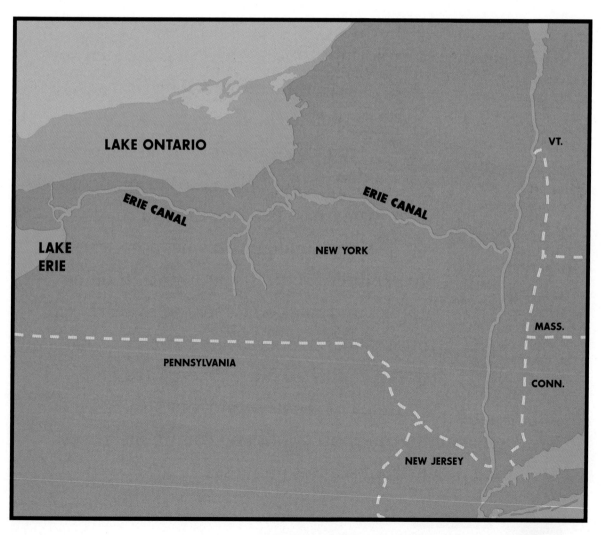

Horses were used on canals in the same way for thousands of years.

CANALS ARE ANCIENT

Canal building is ancient, going back perhaps 5,000 years. The most ancient canals known were along the Euphrates River in Mesopotamia (now Iraq, Iran, and Syria). Famous canals include the Panama Canal and the Suez Canal. The United States built the Panama Canal in 10 years (1904-1914). It allowed ocean travelers to cut 8,000 miles (12,900 km) off the journey around the tip of South America. The 100-mile (160-km) long Suez Canal, which links the Red Sea with the Mediterranean, is 190 feet (58 m) wide at the surface and at least 33 feet (10 m) deep. The French dug it by hand over nearly a century (1805-1894).

The Panama Canal during its construction

Chapter II: THE BARRIERS OF GEOGRAPHY

In 1783, when the American Revolution ended, the region of the five Great Lakes was still largely out of the reach of Americans. This area was important to the new country's defenses, trade and industry, and settlement. It included a major boundary between the United States and British and French colonies (now Canada), splitting four of the five

A major obstacle barring easy access to the Great Lakes was Niagara Falls.

lakes in half. But among existing states, only the unsettled portions of New York, Pennsylvania, and the new state of Ohio bordered on any of the Great Lakes. The lakes were part of the vast and largely empty Northwest Territory, about 300,000 square miles (776,700 square km) of land acquired by the United States at the end of the Revolutionary War.

Map of the Northwest Territory, which was mostly unsettled in 1787.

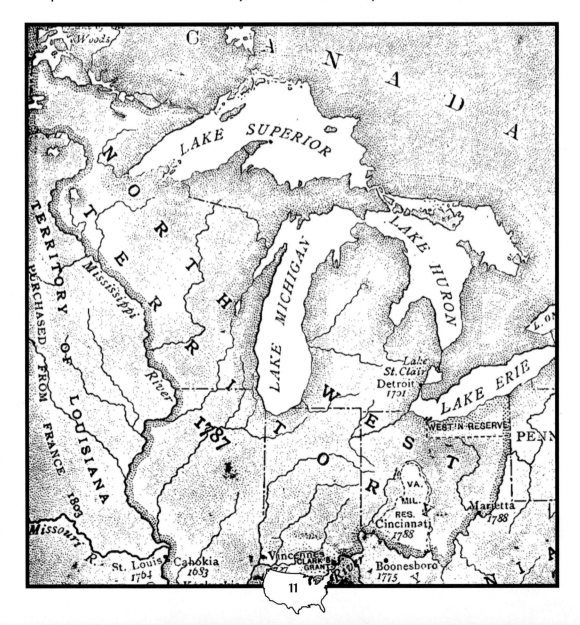

This heavily forested region had been a rich center of fur trapping and trading by the Dutch, British, and French since the 17th century. Before that, Native American tribes had hunted and lived there for centuries. The states of Ohio, Indiana, Illinois, Michigan, Wisconsin, and part of Minnesota would eventually be formed from the Northwest Territory. But in 1783, just reaching the Great Lakes took weeks or months, depending on the weather. The lakes were only accessible by boat from Canada, using the St. Lawrence River.

The canal allowed the nation to tap into natural resources such as bass from the Great Lakes.

Men shown here poling along the Mohawk River. Few boats had sails, and wind was unreliable.

American travelers could take a boat up the Hudson River 150 miles (241 km) to Albany, then carry belongings and trade goods by mule-drawn wagon a dozen miles (19 km) to the Mohawk River. They would then **pole** along the Mohawk another 100 miles (161 km), travel overland again, and finally reach Lake Ontario. However, that journey was slow and difficult and the cliffs of Niagara Falls blocked passage into Lake Erie. A canal to the Great Lakes would make it easier to settle and supply the region, making its rich resources such as fish, game, timber, and minerals available to growing colonial America.

President
George Washington

To America's first president, **George Washington**, there was another good reason to build a canal. The new United States was very loosely organized and as yet had no central government. The people of the southern states were used to trading with the Spanish and French, who still claimed Florida and the territories west of the Mississippi.

Americans settling along the northern Mississippi Valley traded with the French and British in Canada. Distance and geographical obstacles such as the Appalachian Mountains discouraged settlers from trading with their eastern **compatriots**. Trading relationships were all important, allowing people to survive and prosper. President Washington and others worried that western and northern groups of Americans might try to join Spain or Canada or even form independent nations. A canal joining the Atlantic with the Great Lakes would tie the nation together and encourage the economic growth of these western hinterlands.

CANADA

LAKE ONTARIO

LAKE
ERIE

NEW YORK

HUDSON RIVER

PENNSYLVANIA

APPALACHIAN MOUNTAINS

WASHINGTON,
D.C.

ATLANTIC OCEAN

15

Chapter III: AN EXPERIMENT IN ENGINEERING

The Erie Canal was not America's first canal, but it was the country's first major man-made **navigational** waterway. Older projects included a small canal dug in 1730 near Utica, New York, and minor canals in Pennsylvania and Maryland. But the Erie, built by New York State from 1817 to 1825, was a major accomplishment in American history. Its success is especially admirable given the lack of canal-building knowledge in the country at the time. The Erie Canal marked the beginning of **civil engineering** as a profession in the United States and also led to the invention of **hydraulic** cement.

NAME OF THE CANAL

The name *Erie* comes from the Erie Indians, or "Cat Nation," an **Iroquoian**-speaking tribe of the New York-Pennsylvania region. They were almost wiped out in the middle of the 17th century, and the survivors became part of the **Seneca** tribe.

Engraving of Iroquois Chieftain Hiawatha

GEOLOGY

In the 1820s, very little was known about the **geology** of the state. A private citizen who was also a canal **commissioner**, **Stephen Van Rensselaer**, hired a well-known geologist, **Amos Eaton**, to conduct a scientific survey of the route. He published his results in 1824, and it still is considered an important document classifying the rocks of New York State.

In 1824 Congress authorized the Army Engineers to survey America's roads and canals.

DeWitt Clinton

In 1724, **Cadwallader Colden** was the first to propose building the Erie Canal along its present route. Others talked of different approaches and suggested ways of funding **surveys**, but nothing was approved until 1792, when the New York legislature passed an act "for establishing and opening **lock** navigation within the state." In 1804, **Simeon DeWitt**, **surveyor general** of New York, talked about connecting the Hudson River with the Great Lakes via a canal through the Mohawk Valley. His cousin, **DeWitt Clinton**, who became New York's governor in 1817, had led a **lobbying** effort to plan the canal. Once he was in office, the funding was quickly approved. But many people thought it would be a failure—even President Jefferson was skeptical. Clinton's **political** opponents nicknamed the future canal "Clinton's Big Ditch."

Although canals had been built in Europe for centuries, America had neither canal engineers nor skilled construction workers. In 1817 Governor Clinton sent a young surveyor, **Canvass White**, to Europe to study canal-building techniques, materials, and tools. White walked 2,000 miles (3,220 km) inspecting canals in England and Holland. He returned in 1818 with modern surveying tools and drawings of bridges, **aqueducts**, and **culverts** he had studied.

Men working on the Hudson River

HYDRAULIC CEMENT

Hydraulic cement is essential to canal and bridge construction because it hardens and bonds underwater. Canvass White found that the **limestone** used by the English to waterproof canals was too expensive to import. He experimented with native limestone and other materials and invented a hydraulic cement that was both cheaper and better than the English version. More than 500,000 **bushels** (18,000 cu m) were used to build the Erie Canal. After White patented his discovery in 1820, it was used throughout the United States and also exported abroad.

Benjamin Wright

Three engineers were named to build the canal—**Benjamin Wright**, **James Geddes**, and **David S. Bates**. They had some schooling in law and surveying, but were largely self-taught. They drew the plans, designed the locks and aqueducts, and supervised construction. Today, Wright, the canal's chief engineer, is recognized as the "father of civil engineering" in America. Bates and Geddes worked under Wright as assistant engineers for the route's different sections. Canvass White headed the surveying team for a major part of the route.

This illustration of Rochester, New York, shows some of the features of the Erie Canal.

LOCKS

A canal lock is like a watertight box, and a series of locks is like a stairway of water. Since a ship or barge cannot take steps, the "stairs" themselves change levels. If a ship is moving downwards, it sits in a lock, or box, while **sluices** in the lower gates allow water to move into the lock below. When the water level is equal in both locks, the ship can pass through the gate into the next lock and the process continues. If the ship is moving up the lock, water flows into the lock from the sluice above until the two "stairs" are level. Then, the vessel can pass through the gate, "climbing the stairs."

The balance beam (A) opened or closed the main gate; the sluice gate (B) and its control (C) permitted water to flow slowly into or out of a lock. This procedure allowed a boat to be raised or lowered to the level of the water outside the exit gate. The sluice gate was locked and sealed against the miter sill (D).

The $7 million to build the canal was raised by banks buying **bonds** issued by the State of New York. When the canal began to collect **tolls** from its users, part of that money went back to the State, which gradually paid off the bonds with **dividends** for the **investors**. Within nine years, the canal had paid back its original cost, and in less than 20 years, the bonds (plus dividends) were all paid off.

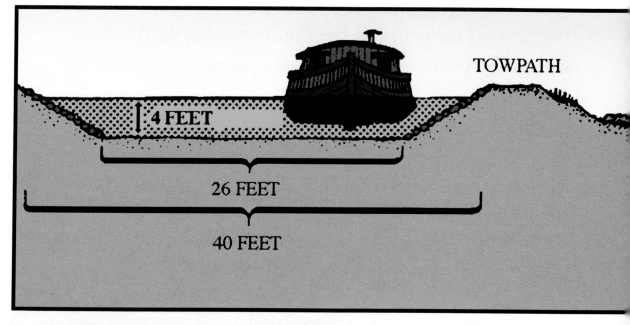

TOWPATH

4 FEET

26 FEET

40 FEET

(Above) diagram shows the required dimensions of the canal and size of boat. The canal often ran at a higher elevation than the river, and boats had to be raised and lowered in the locks. (Left) the five double locks at Lockport, originally constructed in 1824, have since been enlarged.

CANAL CONSTRUCTION

A canal has to be built in level sections. Where there are significant elevation changes, a lock or a series of locks is constructed to raise or lower the canal. If the canal must cross a road or railroad, the usual solution is to build a bridge. When another waterway is encountered, either it or the new canal is placed on an aqueduct. It is important to prevent **seepage** of canal water into the ground, so canals are often lined. Early canals were lined with clay but today choices include **tarry** materials, sheet **polyethylene**, and concrete. Special lining machines can lay wet concrete in an even layer for many miles.

RIVER

The design of this canal shows the great effort made in its lining.

Chapter IV: THE INCREDIBLE FEAT OF BUILDING THE CANAL

With great **fanfare**, on July 4, 1817, untrained crews began digging with picks, shovels, and box-like scoops, moving dirt in wheelbarrows. Work began at Rome, N.Y., moving westward toward Buffalo. Rome was chosen as the starting place because for 80 miles (129 km), the ground was level enough that locks would not be needed. Also, no rivers were in the way that would present the need for bridges or aqueducts. Therefore, Governor Clinton could get a good start on this immense undertaking and calm the doubts that many citizens had voiced about its chances for success.

Thousands of workers dug large parts of the canal and moved tons of dirt by hand.

Mosquitoes carried disease and were a large health risk to canal workers.

Many of the workers were English, Irish, and Welsh **immigrants**. They earned $12 per month plus lodging and meals. About 1,200 laborers dug as deep as 30 feet (9.1 m) in solid stone, hauling out debris by hand and later using horse-powered cranes. They created 70-foot (21-m) high stone heaps, which still could be seen a century later. When they came to the Niagara **escarpment**, next to Niagara Falls, they built double locks to lift boats in five giant steps. (Double locks let boat traffic pass in both directions at the same time.)

RISKS OF BUILDING THE CANAL

With the exception of places where black gunpowder was used to blast through rock formations, all 363 miles (584 km) were built by the muscle power of men and horses. The workers were at great risk of contracting **malaria**, among other hazards, because much of the work took place in dense forests with mosquito-filled swamps and creeks. In 1819 alone, more than 1,000 men were disabled by malaria, and a number of them died. Rattlesnakes were also a constant danger.

An aerial view of the stone Erie Canal aqueduct in Rochester, New York

When completed, the Erie Canal was 363 miles (584 km) long, 40 feet (12 m) wide, and four feet (1.2 m) deep. It rose a total of 568 feet (173 m) in **elevation** over its entire length. It had 84 locks, 90 feet by 15 feet (27 by 4.6 m), and 18 aqueducts. The aqueducts, built of stone, were engineering marvels. One, over the Genesee River, was 802 feet (244 m) long, supported on piles, with 11 limestone arches.

QUICKSAND

To carry the Erie Canal over the Irondequoit Creek near Rochester, a 245-foot (74.7-m) long stone aqueduct was required. But the soil in the area was **quicksand**. The aqueduct was placed on more than 900 wooden piles, one foot (0.3 m) thick and 12 to 20 feet (3.7 to 6 m) long. These were driven into the sand to support the aqueduct.

GRAND CANAL CELEBRATION

This engraving was printed to celebrate the opening of the Erie Canal. It was printed by a group of rope makers.

Sections of the Erie Canal were opened to boat traffic as they were completed, always with much ceremony. In 1819, the first section opened between Rome and Utica, with water flowing down the canal from Lake Erie carrying a boat with a military band playing on its deck. As it passed, crowds cheered from the banks. On July 4, 1820, the 96-mile (154-km) long middle section opened. It was exactly three years from the day the work started, and excitement was high. Hundreds of people arrived from towns along the canal, joining together in 73 boats near Syracuse. As they waved colorful banners, officials gave speeches. Then the procession moved single-file down the canal to Salina, where festivities continued.

(Left) a barge loaded with grain rides the current of the canal. (Below) painting of the aqueduct bridge at Rochester by James Eights, 1824

More ceremonies were held in October 1823, when the section to Albany was completed. Most of the critics had been silenced by this time. On October 26, 1825, eight years after it was begun, the entire Erie Canal was officially opened. Newspapers called the opening "a cultural event of the first **magnitude**." Festivals were held throughout the

state, and a procession of people 5 miles (8 km) long marched through the streets of New York City toward the harbor to receive the arriving fleet of **canal boats**. In Buffalo, on Lake Erie, crowds gathered to see the boats off. The fleet left Buffalo, traveled the 363 miles (584 km) to Albany on the Hudson River, and continued down the Hudson to New York City. The total distance was 425 miles (684 km), and the trip took 10 days. People ate on the boats and slept in men's or women's **dormitories** in bunk beds that were only 18 inches (46 cm) wide. Because of the excitement, few actually slept. One boat, called "Noah's Ark," carried a live bear, two eagles, two fawns, and several fish, along with two Native American boys.

Entrance of the canal into the Hudson at Albany (James Eights, 1824)

The opening of the Erie Canal occurred before any telegraph network was in place, so planners came up with a clever way to let all of New York know the boats were coming. They placed cannons along the entire canal route, each cannon being within hearing distance of the next. When the boats were launched, the first cannon was fired, signaling the next to fire, and so on. It took the cannon signal one and a half hours to reach New York City, and then it was sent booming back to Buffalo.

Crowds lined the banks of the Erie Canal and cheered the fleet on its journey. As the boats entered each town, an official greeter was waiting with three questions, which were answered by people on the lead boat.

THE QUESTIONS

The greeter asked, "Who comes there?" Answer: "Your brothers from the West, on the waters of the Great Lakes." Question: "By what means have they been diverted so far from their natural course?" Answer: "Through the channel of the Erie Canal." Question: "By whose authority and by whom was a work of such magnitude accomplished?" Answer: "By the authority and the **enterprise** of the people of the State of New York."

A proud Governor Clinton and other **dignitaries** were aboard a **packet boat** called *Seneca Chief*. As the fleet arrived in New York Harbor on November 4, 1825, other beautifully decorated boats joined the procession. The fleet formed a circle near Sandy Hook, where Governor Clinton emptied two casks of water from Lake Erie into the Atlantic Ocean. This celebration was called the "Marriage of the Waters." Then, **Dr. Samuel Mitchell** poured bottles of water he had collected from many rivers all over the world into New York Harbor. Water from the Ganges in India, the Seine in France, the Amazon in South America, the Columbia in the Pacific Northwest, and other rivers mingled with Atlantic waters to **symbolize** the **commerce** that New York planned to carry out with all nations.

A mural by C.Y. Turner, 1905, depicts Governor DeWitt Clinton at the ceremony celebrating the "Marriage of the Waters" in 1825.

Cannons boomed along the canal signaling its opening.

At day's end, lights were turned on in thousands of public buildings and private residences all over New York, and the city put on the greatest display of fireworks its citizens had ever seen. When the fleet returned up the canal to Buffalo, many people carried kegs of Atlantic Ocean water to pour into Lake Erie.

The canal was hailed as a great engineering achievement. It cut the travel time from New York Harbor to Lake Erie in half and reduced shipping costs by 94 percent. Before the canal was built, freight between Buffalo and New York City cost $90 to $125 a ton ($80 to $115 per metric ton). Ten years later, using the Erie Canal, freight cost $4 a ton ($3.65 per metric ton).

Fireworks were launched at the opening ceremony of the canal, which inspired many artistic interpretations.

Even before its opening, more than 8,000 men with 2,000 boats and 9,000 horses or mules were employed on the Erie Canal. Almost overnight, New York City became the nation's busiest port and the main gateway to the Northwest Territory.

(Above) the canal provided thousands of people with much-needed jobs, such as operating the locks.
(Below) postcard showing life on the Erie Canal, Durhamville, New York

Modern aqueduct on part of the Erie Canal, Rochester, New York

The opening of the Erie Canal triggered the first great westward migration of settlers. Within 10 years, the town of Rochester had become the nation's first "**boom town**," increasing its population from 300 to 8,000. Other towns along the canal such as Rome, Troy, Utica, Lockport, and Buffalo also grew quickly.

HOW THE POPULATION CHANGED

Canal and railroad construction created a huge demand for cheap labor. During the 1820s, 129,000 foreigners entered the country, increasing to 540,000 in the 1830s. Of that number, 44% were Irish, 30% were German, and 15% English. Immigration tripled in the 1840s, rising to 2,814,554 during the 1850s. Meanwhile, the total population of the United States more than doubled over 30 years, increasing from 9,600,000 in 1820 to 23,200,000 in 1850.

Following New York's example, other states soon began forming canal **corporations** and building their own canals. Ohio linked the Great Lakes with the Mississippi Valley in 1833-34, permitting barge and boat traffic as far as New Orleans. Pennsylvania built a system of canals to Pittsburgh, which meant having to cross the Allegheny Mountains at an elevation of 2,300 feet (700 m). By 1840, Pennsylvania had almost 1,000 miles (1,600 km) of canal in operation.

TYPICAL FREIGHT COSTS

In 1820, when canal sections first opened, boats carried flour or grain for one cent per ton per mile. Firewood could be carried for one cent per **cord** per mile, and fence posts for two cents per thousand per mile. A person traveled for five cents per mile. Salt, which was mined near Buffalo, was brought to the city for a half cent per ton per mile.

TABLE OF THE NEW RATES OF TOLL
ON THE ERIE CANAL,

As established by the Canal board, and in effect on said Canal.

Produce, &c.   Merchandize Furn't.

Miles.		Toll of a bbl Flour.	100 lbs 4. m.	100 lbs 3. m.	100 lbs 2. m.	100 lbs 1. m.	Miles.		100 lbs 8. m.	100 lbs 5. m.	100 lbs 3. m.
		C M F	C M F	C M F	C M F	C M F			C M F	C M F	C M F
0	BUFFALO.						0	ALBANY.			
3	Black Rock,......	0 2 5.9.0	0 1 2	0 0 9	0 0 6	0 0 3	5	Port Schuyler,.....	0 4 0	0 2 5	0 1 5
4	Lower Black Rock,	0 3 4.5.6	0 1 6	0 1 2	0 0 8	0 0 4	6	Gibbonsville,......	0 4 8	0 3 0	0 1 8
12	Tonawanda,......	1 0 3.6.8	0 4 8	0 3 6	0 2 4	0 1 2	7	West Troy,......	0 5 6	0 3 5	0 2 1
18	H. Brockway's,....	1 5 5.5.2	0 7 2	0 5 4	0 3 6	0 1 8	10	Cohoes, ...	0 8 0	0 5 0	0 3 0
23	Welch's, ...	1 9 8.7.2	0 9 2	0 6 9	0 4 6	0 2 3	13	Lower Aqueduct,...	1 0 4	0 6 5	0 3 9
24	Pendleton,........	2 0 7.3.6	0 9 6	0 7 6	0 4 8	0 2 4	19	Willow Spring,....	1 5 2	0 9 5	0 5 7
31	Lockport,........	2 6 7.8.4	1 2 4	0 9 3	0 6 2	0 3 1	26	Upper Aqueduct,....	2 0 8	1 3 0	0 7 8
37	Orange Port,......	3 1 9.6.8	1 4 8					Schenectady,......	2 4 0	1 5 0	0 9 0
38	Gasport,.........	3 2 8.3.2	1 5 2				39	Rotterdam,........	3 1 2	1 9 5	1 1 7
40	Reynold's Basin,...	3 4 5.6.0	1 6 0				44	Phillip's Locks,...	3 5 2	2 2 0	1 3 2
43	Middleport, ...	3 7 1.5.2	1 7 2	1 2 9 0			45	Florida,.........	3 6 0	2 2 5	1 3 5
46	Shelby Basin, ...	3 9 7.4.4	1 8 4	1 3 8	0 9 2	0 4 6	47	Amsterdam, ...	3 7 6	2 3 5	1 4 1

But in 1826 the first railroad in the United States, a small horse-drawn line, opened between Milton and Quincy, Massachusetts. It marked the beginning of the end of canals as a principal means of heavy transportation. By 1850, a railroad system connected New York City with Buffalo, Philadelphia, and Pittsburgh, and in 1856 Chicago was added to the network. Freight companies quickly moved their business to railroads, which were faster and superior overall—especially in winter, when canals were subject to freezing.

Before the canal was expanded, it was shallow and would freeze when winter weather hit. The ice made the canal unusable, and sometimes boats would get trapped in the ice like the *Hartford Socony*, shown here.

(Left) men working on canal bridge construction, 1908. (Right) bridge construction, 1909

The Erie Canal was enlarged in 1862 and continued to build in traffic, reaching its peak in the 1880s. It was expanded twice more in 1895 and 1918. After that, it was used less and began to decline. In 1903 it was incorporated into the New York State Barge Canal system. This system, now called the New York State Canal System, includes the Champlain, Oswego, and Cayuga and Seneca canals, which connect Lake Erie with other lakes in the area. Today, the canal system is more than 524 miles (843 km) long. More than 70 percent of New York state residents live within 2 miles (3.25 km) of the canal system's waterways.

CLINTON'S PREDICTION

Governor Clinton worked hard to convince the New York legislature to fund the Erie Canal. He predicted that the city would become "...the **granary** of the world, the **emporium** of commerce, the seat of manufactures... and before the **revolution** of a century, the whole island of Manhattan, covered with inhabitants and replenished with a dense population, will constitute one vast city." This prediction came true. In 1829, 3,640 bushels (131 cu m) of wheat came down the canal from Buffalo, and after only 12 years, the figure had increased to one million bushels (36,000 cu m). Meanwhile the population of New York City had grown from about 200,000 in 1825 to almost 700,000 in 1850.

The canal was influential in the quick growth of New York State. Genesee River view, New York, 1914

Emblem marking 175 years of the Erie Canal

In the 20th century, the canal network became more of a recreational and historic resource than a transportation corridor. In 2001, this network was designated the nation's 23rd National Heritage Corridor. People can launch their own boat or rent a boat and visit cities and towns along the canal. Vessels up to 300 feet (91 m) long and 40 feet (12 m) wide can travel the canal, but bridges limit overhead clearance to 15-1/2 feet (4.7 m) in some places and 20 feet (6 m) in others. The historic towns along the route sponsor summer festivals. In Medina, motorists can drive under the Erie Canal, and in Lockport, a **powerhouse** that once ran the locks and two lift bridges is now a canal museum. The five locks that once carried boats up the Niagara cliffs are now used only as a **spillway**, having been replaced by dual locks that lift boats 50 feet (15 m) to the level of Lake Erie. Today the Erie Canal has only 57 locks.

"LOW BRIDGE" SONG

In 1913, a well-known song about the Erie Canal was written down. It is about the "**canawlers**'" resistance to engine-driven barges, which were replacing their mules that had traditionally walked along the banks, pulling the barges.

I've got a mule, her name is Sal
Fifteen years on the Erie Canal.
She's a good ol' worker and a good ol' pal
Fifteen years on the Erie Canal.
We've hauled some barges in our day
Filled with lumber, coal, and hay
And we know every inch of the way
From Albany to Buffalo.

Chorus: **Low bridge**, everybody down
Low bridge, for we're comin' to a town
And you'll always know your neighbor
You'll always know your pal
If you've ever navigated on the Erie Canal.

Poster showing sheet music for the song "Low Bridge, Everybody Down" by Thomas S. Allen, 1913

We better get on our way, old pal
Fifteen years on the Erie Canal.
'Cause you bet your life I'd never part with Sal
Fifteen years on the Erie Canal.
Get up there mule, here comes a lock
We'll make Rome 'bout six o'clock
One more trip and back we'll go
Right back home to Buffalo.

(Repeat chorus.)

Some versions of the song substitute "fifteen miles" for "fifteen years."

A man unloads a horse from a canal boat, Rochester, 1915.

Key People in the History of THE ERIE CANAL

Bates, David S. - New York engineer on the middle division of the Erie Canal.

Clinton, DeWitt - (1769-1828) Nephew of George Clinton, New York governor; mayor of New York City 1803-1815, and chief promoter of the Erie Canal.

Colden, Cadwallader - (1688-1776) Political leader of New York; appointed surveyor-general in 1721.

DeWitt, Simeon - (1768-1836) Map-maker for George Washington and surveyor-general of New York State for many years.

Eaton, Amos - (1776-1842) New York lawyer and scientist who surveyed the geology of the Erie Canal route (1822-23).

Geddes, James - (1763-1838) Self-trained engineer and surveyor; also served as a judge and New York legislator.

Jefferson, Thomas - (1743-1826) Third president of the United States (1801-1809).

Mitchell, Dr. Samuel - A well-known New York physician.

Van Rensselaer, Stephen - (1764-1839) New York congressman (1822-29) and president of the New York State Canal Commission (1825-31).

Washington, George - (1732-1799) First president of the United States (1789-1797).

White, Canvass - (1790-1834) Chief surveyor on the Erie Canal.

Wright, Benjamin - (1770-1842) Chief engineer on the Erie Canal. In 1970, the American Society of Civil Engineers named him the Father of Civil Engineering.

(Right) Amos Eaton

43

A Timeline of the History of
THE ERIE CANAL

1724	A canal is proposed to link Lake Erie and the Hudson River.
1792	New York legislature authorizes lock navigation in the state.
1798	The Niagara Canal Company is incorporated to build a canal between Lake Ontario and Lake Erie.
1808	New York State Legislature authorizes a survey of possible canal routes.
1817	New York State Legislature authorizes $7 million to build a canal from Albany to Buffalo. Governor DeWitt Clinton breaks ground for the canal.
1819	First boat travels the Erie Canal from Rome to Utica.
1825	The Erie Canal opens along its full length with statewide festivities and ceremonies.
1826-1856	Building of railroads begins to make the canal obsolete.
1836-1862	The Erie Canal is widened to 70 feet (21 m), deepened to 7 feet (2.1 m), and 72 double locks are added.
1882	Tolls are abolished on the canal, which has already raised more than $113 million over its original cost.
1895	Second enlargement of the canal is approved, deepening it to a minimum depth of 9 feet (2.7 m).

1903-1918   Third enlargement of the Erie Canal, as authorized by the Barge Canal Act. The work combines the Erie, Champlain, Oswego, and Cayuga and Seneca canals into the New York State Barge Canal System at a cost of $155 million. The Barge Canal's western end is changed from Buffalo to Tonawanda. Its eastern end changes from Albany to Waterford.

1995   Creation of the Canal Recreationway Commission, a 24-member body to advise the state on canal-related activities.

1996   A $32 million, five-year Canal Revitalization Program is developed to preserve and rehabilitate the canal and to enhance recreational opportunities.

2001   The Canal System is named the nation's 23rd National Heritage Corridor.

Canal boat family at Lock 37, 1880s

GLOSSARY

aqueduct - A structure that carries a canal across another body of water.

bond - A paper that represents money owed; a piece of paper sold to raise money that will be paid back in the future with dividends.

boom town - A town that is experiencing rapid growth in business and population.

bushel - Unit of dry weight, equal to about eight gallons, used mainly for grains.

canal boats - Flat-bottomed boats, such as barges, used on artificial waterways to transport goods.

canawler - Immigrants' pronunciation of canaler (a man who worked on a canal).

civil engineering - A branch of engineering that involves design and construction, especially of public works such as roads, canals, dams, and utilities.

commerce - The buying and selling (including transportation) of goods.

commissioner - A member of a commission; group of people assigned to perform a duty.

compatriot - A citizen of the same country.

continental - Relating to or typical of a continent.

cord - A stack of wood cut for fuel that is 128 cubic feet (3.58 cubic m)

corporation - A legally organized group of one or more persons authorized to act as a single person.

culvert - A drain that lies crosswise to the main route.

dignitary - One who has a high rank.

dividend - A share, often of money, distributed among shareholders.

dormitory - A room for sleeping.

elevation - Height above the level of the sea.

emporium - Commercial center; department store or shopping mall.

enterprise - Business; a difficult or risky project.

escarpment - A long cliff or steep slope produced by erosion or earthquake activity.

fanfare - A showy outward display.

geology - The science of the history of the Earth, especially as recorded in rocks.

granary - A storehouse for grain.

hinterland - A region lying inland, remote from any coast and far from cities.

hydraulic - Relating to water or other moving liquid.

immigrant - A person who moves into a country from somewhere else.

investor - A person who commits money to earn additional money.

Iroquoian - A Native language of eastern North America.

limestone - A rock formed of calcium carbonate, the remains of shells or coral.

lobby - To try to influence public officials, especially members of government.

lock - An enclosure with gates used to raise or lower boats moving through a waterway.

"low bridge" - The warning cry to hit the deck because the canal boat was about to pass under a bridge. Bridges were built low to save money.

magnitude - Size, extent, or importance.

malaria - A human disease caused by parasites in the red blood cells and spread by the bites of mosquitoes.

navigational - Relating to getting ships or aircraft from place to place.

packet boat - A sleek passenger boat.

pole - To propel a boat with a pole.

political - Relating to government, especially the making of government policy.

polyethylene - A lightweight plastic created chemically with heat, resistant to chemicals and moisture.

powerhouse - An electrical power plant.

quicksand - A type of sand that gives way to pressure, in which heavy objects tend to sink.

revolution - Turning; the time it takes to make a complete turn, for example of a planet around the sun.

seepage - Oozing or seeping, as through porous material.

Seneca - A member of a Native American group who lived in what is now western New York.

sluice - An artificial passage for water with a valve or gate to regulate flow.

spillway - A passage for surplus water to run over or around a dam or other obstruction.

surveyor general - One who is in charge of those who survey land, for example for an entire state.

survey - To determine the form, extent, and position of a tract of land by using instruments that measure angles and lines.

symbolize - To represent or express by a symbol, or sign.

tarry - Made of or similar to tar.

territory - A geographical area; in the United States, an area under its control, with a separate legislature, but not yet a state.

toll - A tax or fee paid for some liberty or privilege, for example passing through a canal.

transcontinental - Extending across a continent, such as a railway.

Books of Interest

Harness, Cheryl. *The Amazing, Impossible Erie Canal*, Simon & Schuster, 1995.

Larkin, F. Daniel. *New York State Canals: a Short History*, Purple Mountain Press, Ltd., 1998.

Lourie, Peter. *Erie Canal: Canoeing America's Great Waterway*, Boyds Mills Press, 1999.

McFee, Michele A. *A Long Haul: the Story of the New York State Barge Canal*, Purple Mountain Press, Ltd., 1999.

Panagopoulos, Janie L. *Erie Trail West: A Dream-Quest Adventure*, River Road Publications, 2003.

Santella, Andrew. *The Erie Canal*, Compass Point Books, 2004.

Stein, R. Conrad. *The Erie Canal*, Children's Press, 2004.

Web Sites

http://www.westernny.com/erie.html

http://www.nycanal.com/nycanalhistory.html

http://www.canals.state.ny.us/cculture/history/

http://www.nyhistory.com/links/Erie_Canal.htm

http://canals.org/

http://www.syracuse.com/features/eriecanal/

http://www.history.rochester.edu/canal/

INDEX

Linda Thompson is a Montana native and a graduate of the University of Washington. She was a teacher, writer, and editor in the San Francisco Bay Area for 30 years and now lives in Taos, New Mexico. She can be contacted through her web site,

http://www.highmesaproductions.com